LINES IN THE SAND

Building Boundaries with Grace

This book is intended for educational and informational purposes only. It is not a substitute for professional mental health, medical, or legal advice. The author and publisher disclaim any liability arising directly or indirectly from the use or application of the information contained in this book.

ISBN: 979-8-218-92283-2

Published by Dr. Ness Says

Printed in the United States of America

AUTHOR BIO

Dr. Tonnessa L. Gibson, a Board-Certified Licensed Professional Counselor with over 16 years of experience, empowers individuals and families to overcome life's challenges. She holds a Doctorate in Counseling Education from Texas Southern University and a Master's degree in General Counseling and Guidance from Louisiana Tech University. Dr. Gibson's extensive academic knowledge, combined with her practical expertise across diverse counseling settings, enables her to provide specialized support in crisis intervention, stress management, mindfulness, and coping strategies. She is committed to serving clients from various ethnic, cultural, and developmental backgrounds, fostering resilience and well-being in the face of adversity.

Her holistic approach integrates evidence-based techniques with empathy and compassion, creating a safe and supportive space for personal growth and healing. Through her work, Dr. Gibson has touched the lives of many, guiding them toward greater self-awareness, emotional balance, and lasting change.

BOOK DESCRIPTION

In a world that often demands more than we can give, *Lines in the Sand* offers a gentle yet powerful guide to creating healthy, respectful boundaries. Whether in relationships, work, or personal life, establishing boundaries is key to preserving your mental, emotional, and physical well-being.

This eBook empowers you to set boundaries with confidence, without guilt or fear, and teaches you how to communicate with grace and compassion. It explores the importance of saying "no" when necessary, understanding your limits, and fostering mutual respect in every interaction.

Lines in the Sand shows you how to navigate life's challenges while maintaining your peace and authenticity. If you're ready to reclaim your time, energy, and sense of self, this book will be your trusted guide to living a balanced, fulfilling life.

TABLE OF CONTENTS

INTRODUCTION

Personal Boundaries

Setting personal boundaries is essential to establishing healthy relationships. These boundaries define the fundamental principles for how you wish to be regarded.

The issue with boundary violators is that they are unaware of the definition of a boundary. It is up to you to instruct them regarding your boundaries, particularly when it comes to your mental health and well-being.

Boundaries are fundamental, respectful guidelines that dictate how others should conduct themselves in your presence. This should be self-evident, right? If you are reading this, you may be someone who respects boundaries but has been perplexed by how you have been treated by a friend, coworker, loved one, or family member. You may be seeking a way to address the peculiar emotions you are experiencing about someone infringing upon your emotional, physical, or psychological boundaries. One method of determining whether you are being violated is to trust your intuition and distress, as they are likely accurate.

Setting boundaries necessitates practice. It entails determining what behavior is acceptable and what is not and deciding how to respond if someone exceeds your comfort zone. You can develop mutually respectful, appropriate, and compassionate relationships by establishing boundaries. We have all experienced the sensation of our boundaries being violated at some point. Some indicators may include the feeling that a person is "strange," "disrespectful," or "creepy" when interacting with them. They may deny that they said or told you something, which may cause you to doubt your rationality. Such situations can result in distress, whether it is a stranger standing too close to you or touching you (physical boundary) or someone asking very personal questions (emotional boundary). You may have been the victim of emotional abuse or discrimination in the workplace or school (psychological). All are instances of boundary violations.

We often assume that others will respect our boundaries because we were taught what is considered acceptable by our family and/or culture. Regrettably, this is not always the case. While we can choose the people we interact with in our personal lives—such as close companions—this choice is often limited in work, family, or community settings. Interacting with those who maintain inadequate boundaries can lead to feelings of discomfort or even violation. In particular, people with mental health conditions may face additional challenges in protecting their boundaries. Often, we become aware that our boundaries have been breached through how we feel. Feelings of confusion, anxiety, or exhaustion in the presence of someone may signal that our boundaries have been crossed. Therefore, we must be aware of the strategies for establishing healthy emotional, psychological, and physical boundaries in relationships to experience a sense of safety and respect. How do we do this? The initial step is to be aware of your entitlements to a healthy relationship.

Establishing healthy boundaries begins with recognizing your boundaries in relationships. What constitutes appropriate conduct in a romantic partnership, friendship, or workplace? For instance, if you inform a new acquaintance that you are preoccupied but they persist in contacting you via phone and text, this may signal that they are not amenable to a negative response. A person who consistently disregards your "no" is infringing upon your boundaries. The subsequent step is to adhere to the established boundaries and have a contingency plan in place should someone violate them. This may include setting repercussions if someone exceeds these thresholds. Counseling can also be beneficial if you need help establishing healthy boundaries and developing assertiveness.

I use diverse methods, such as assertiveness counseling, training, and psychoeducation, to help clients establish boundaries effectively. Boundary violations may pose a risk for those who lack assertiveness skills and do not want to be perceived as mean, as they are hesitant to harm someone's emotions and prioritize their own needs. In addition, clients may require assistance when their boundaries have been violated (e.g., due to physical assault, sexual assault, or abuse) and are experiencing emotional trauma, such as anxiety or depression, as a consequence of their ordeal.

Why Boundaries?

Those who struggle to prioritize their needs may overlook the importance of boundaries in terms of their mental health and overall well-being. If you identify with this, it is time to implement significant changes. Boundaries safeguard not only your integrity but also every aspect of your well-being.

Prioritizing Self-Care

Prioritizing self-care is vital for preserving your mental health and overall well-being. It involves participating in activities that foster tension reduction, relaxation, and overall well-being. Nevertheless, this can be challenging when you are perpetually striving to satisfy the requirements of others. This is the point at which boundaries are crucial. By setting clear boundaries, you create the necessary time and space to practice self-care. This may entail declining specific requests or taking time off work to recuperate and rejuvenate.

Developing Positive Relationships

Healthy relationships are built on mutual respect and trust. Clear boundaries facilitate the communication of acceptable and unacceptable conduct to others. This clarity can help you develop positive relationships with your family, acquaintances, and colleagues. Establishing boundaries creates a secure environment where you can engage in candid and open communication.

Stress Management

While stress is a natural aspect of life, chronic stress can have a detrimental impact on your mental health and overall well-being. Setting boundaries can help manage stress by providing you with the necessary resources to navigate challenging circumstances. For instance, you might set a boundary to take regular breaks throughout the day to recharge if you are experiencing work-related stress. Alternatively, you may establish a boundary to restrict your interactions with a challenging family member.

Developing Self-Esteem

Self-esteem refers to how you perceive your capabilities and self-worth. Setting and maintaining healthy boundaries demonstrates that you value your own needs and emotions. In doing so, you reinforce your self-worth, which in turn strengthens your self-esteem. By adhering to your boundaries, you send a clear message to yourself and others that you are deserving of respect and consideration.

Advice for Establishing Healthy Boundaries

Determine Your Values and Needs

To establish healthy boundaries, you must first identify your values and needs. Take time to contemplate what matters to you most and what you require to experience a sense of security, contentment, and satisfaction. Once you have a comprehensive understanding of your values and needs, you can begin establishing boundaries that align with them.

Demonstrate Clarity and Directness

Communicating your boundaries requires being direct and explicit with others. It entails being clear and assertive about what you are comfortable with. For instance, if a friend requests that you participate in an activity that makes you feel uneasy, you could respond by stating, "I appreciate your invitation, but I am currently prioritizing my self-care and will be unable to attend."

Start Small

Establishing healthy boundaries can be difficult, especially if you are accustomed to prioritizing the needs of others over your own. It is acceptable to start with modest boundaries and gradually expand them. For instance, you could begin by limiting your use of social media for a few hours each day and subsequently increase the time you spend away from it.

Demonstrate Self-Compassion

Setting and upholding healthy boundaries can be challenging if you are used to putting others first. Therefore, it is crucial to cultivate self-compassion and be lenient with yourself as you progress through this process. Mistakes are a natural part of learning, and it is essential to remember that establishing boundaries is not only necessary but also a skill that develops over time.

Maintain a Consistent Approach

Once you have established your boundaries, it is crucial to uphold them consistently. This can be difficult, especially when others are used to overstepping them. Nevertheless, maintaining consistency conveys that your boundaries are significant and cannot be compromised.

Seek Assistance

Seeking support can greatly help in establishing and maintaining boundaries, particularly if you are not used to prioritizing your own needs. Reaching out to a licensed therapist, family member, or trusted friend can help you remain accountable as you navigate this process.

Acquire the Ability to Say "No"

It can be challenging to decline requests, particularly when we are hesitant to disappoint others. Nevertheless, it is crucial to remember that declining an offer does not imply rejecting others but rather prioritizing your requirements. Learning to say "no" can be empowering and is key to establishing healthy boundaries in all aspects of our lives.

Integrated psychotherapy can be a powerful tool in this journey. A therapist can provide a secure and encouraging environment to explore your values, needs, and triggers while helping you develop strategies for setting and maintaining healthy boundaries. Additionally, they can help you recognize any underlying beliefs or behavioral patterns that may be contributing to your inability to establish consistent boundaries. Therapy is also an effective method for addressing anxiety or other mental health issues that may disrupt your daily life.

Chapter

---- ◆ ----

UNDERSTANDING BOUNDARIES

Defining Boundaries in Different Areas of Life

Boundaries are crucial; however, establishing them can be challenging. You frequently struggle to initiate a conversation or effectively convey their requirements to others.

If you are seeking to establish your boundaries, it may be beneficial first to determine the type of boundary you wish to develop.

Emotional Boundaries

Emotional boundaries often pertain to how others interact with and regard us. These boundaries sometimes only become apparent after being breached, which is perfectly normal.

Let us assume that you had an argument with someone who used an unkind term toward you. Once you have both regained composure, the most effective method of establishing an emotional boundary with that person is to:

- Approach them.

- Enquire about the argument.

- Accept responsibility for any role you may have played in the deterioration of the argument.

- Inform them that you are not amenable to name-calling and that you will require them to engage in future conversations without resorting to such behavior.

Physical Boundaries

What is your comfort level surrounding others in your personal space? There are many reasons why someone might not feel at ease with others being in their space. It's best to set this boundary when it's not yet a concern. When you meet an unfamiliar person, politely let them know what you're comfortable with. Do not feel obligated to extend an apology or explain beyond that.

Never forget: Boundaries are beneficial, and you are permitted to establish your own.

Sexual Boundaries

It is always advisable to converse with your companion regarding your sexual boundaries before commencing a new intimate relationship. This conversation can be initiated by stating, "I am eager to advance our relationship, but I would like to pause to discuss the potential next steps." From there, you can express your comfort level and discomfort in an intimate setting.

Professional Boundaries

The most effective way to establish professional boundaries is first to set the tone for your professional conduct. This should indicate the professional demeanor you aspire for others to exhibit when interacting with you.

After that, it is frequently necessary to delay addressing the situation until the boundary has been breached. For example, suppose a colleague behaves demeaning during a meeting. In that case, you may approach them afterward and articulate the reasons why this behavior was intolerable, as well as the behavior you expect from them in the future.

Do not hesitate to involve human resources if a colleague consistently violates your work boundaries.

Personal Boundaries

Suppose you possess a camper that a close acquaintance wishes to rent for a family vacation. You are willing to let them utilize it, but you also want to ensure that they maintain it in the same manner you would.

In this instance, it is entirely permissible to establish your care guidelines in writing, which should include instructions for general maintenance and cleansing. Having these written instructions stored within the camper would provide your friend with a convenient reference while offering more precise definitions of your boundaries.

Time Constraints

Peoples generally fall into two primary categories in terms of time management: those who are chronically tardy and those who believe that tardiness indicates a lack of preparation.

If you are the latter, you may experience a frequent sense of intrusion into your personal space by the former. Nevertheless, this is a straightforward solution to navigate:

- Determine the duration of time you are prepared to wait beyond the scheduled meeting time.

- Grant yourself the discretion to terminate or abandon an appointment if the specified time is not met.

Communicate in advance with someone who is consistently tardy; let them know that you will be departing after a specified period. Nevertheless, endeavor to convey this without sounding accusatory. Recognizing that the two of you possess distinct personalities can be helpful. You are not attempting to alter them; instead, you must establish time constraints for yourself for the simple reason that you are either unable to afford them or do not wish to wait any longer.

Boundaries Are Different for Everybody

Boundaries are universally applicable; however, their establishment depends on the person and the nature of the relationship. People do not set boundaries in the same way or tone with their mothers as they do with their children. Of course, this is not always the case, as one may assume both parties are mature enough to fully understand boundaries. Similarly, boundaries can differ in intimate relationships. Many people did not receive effective instruction on boundary-setting from their families of origin. As a result, they often acquire this skill through interactions with friends, colleagues, and romantic partners. Nevertheless, establishing boundaries with family members can be a distinctive challenge, as it necessitates time and practice to develop a familiar communication style.

When it comes to establishing boundaries, what does it mean to have "a comfortable voice"? Frequently, the process of acquiring the knowledge necessary to establish them appears to be rigid or predetermined. Numerous boundary-setting courses offer formulations that are followed by the phrase "or in your own words." Even this can feel like an additional script for people who have never previously established boundaries. Often, those who spend years in therapy developing boundary-setting skills begin with rigorous approaches, such as physically removing themselves from situations, giving firm refusals, and carefully structuring their statements with "if–then" phrasing. Over time, these interactions become more natural, enabling them to communicate their limits without assigning blame or shifting responsibility to others. Eventually, most people develop a style that is perceived as genuine; however, a few continue to rely on scripted responses in high-pressure situations. While partners may find this endearing, family members might perceive it as frustrating. Nonetheless, this process requires perseverance and practice. The initial phase involves learning to recognize and attend to your boundaries and then expressing them.

Acknowledging that everyone has their limits is the foundation of effective boundary-setting. This involves establishing an emotionally and physically ergonomic environment to the extent that reality permits. Furthermore, these boundaries will produce an assortment of interactions contingent upon the nature of the relationship, which is entirely typical. For instance, the tone and language used to remind an infant to respect personal space are distinct from those used to address an adult who has chosen to recline in an uncomfortable position at a party. Meanwhile, a partner's proximity in public may be considered acceptable within the context of their relationship, provided that it is consistent with the social environment. Similarly, how an old friend interjects with memory during a conversation may differ from that of a colleague who interrupts with an idea. In all cases, context and relationship dynamics matter.

Initially, setting boundaries may feel awkward or excessively rehearsed, but with consistent practice, a sense of comfort will be achieved. Eventually, the inconvenience of "script mode" is replaced by a personalized approach that aligns with the unique dynamics of each relationship. However, this development is contingent upon that crucial first step: establishing boundaries.

Boundaries as a Reflection of Self-Worth

Boundaries are not merely rules people set for their relationships; they directly reflect their self-esteem and self-worth. The boundaries a person establishes in their personal and professional life indicate their expectations for how they should be treated, their emotional needs, and their sense of self-respect. To affirm their value, people create and enforce boundaries that prioritize their well-being and foster relationships that honor their needs and values. In contrast, the absence of boundaries often suggests uncertainty about self-worth, which can lead to behaviors such as emotional exhaustion, fatigue, and people-pleasing.

Self-Respect and Boundaries

Self-respect is fundamentally about acknowledging and honoring your limitations. A person who values themselves understands that their time, energy, and emotions are not infinite resources to be freely given at the expense of their well-being. By establishing boundaries, they communicate to others that their needs are important. For example, someone who recognizes their worth will not tolerate being disrespected, overburdened with responsibilities, or placed in situations that violate their principles. Instead, they assertively articulate their boundaries and ensure they are respected.

Conversely, people who struggle with self-worth may find it difficult to express their needs or decline requests. They might feel guilty for prioritizing themselves or worry that setting boundaries will lead to conflict or rejection. This often results in resentment and frustration from allowing others to dictate their time, emotional availability, or personal space. How a person enforces—or neglects—their boundaries often reflects their internal beliefs about their own value.

Emotional and Physical Health

Establishing boundaries that support physical and emotional well-being is a natural outcome of a strong sense of self-worth. Emotionally, boundaries protect against depletion, manipulation, and toxic relationships. People who value their well-being avoid relationships that leave them feeling drained, taken advantage of, or disregarded. They limit interactions with those who lack empathy and instead prioritize mutually beneficial connections.

Physical boundaries are equally important for maintaining health and preventing exhaustion. For example, those who neglect rest, overextend themselves at work, or fail to maintain a healthy work-life balance often struggle to recognize their worth beyond productivity. When people value themselves, they understand that personal time, self-care, and leisure are as important as external achievements. They prioritize their health, set clear limits on responsibilities, and avoid self-destructive behaviors.

The Fear of Disapproval and Boundaries

Many people hesitate to establish boundaries due to concerns about how others might react. They worry about appearing harsh, complicated, or egotistical. However, the ability to set and maintain boundaries is not about controlling others' perceptions; it is about ensuring that relationships are based on mutual understanding and respect. Those with a strong sense of self-worth recognize that they do not need to compromise their well-being to gain approval. They understand that some people may resist their boundaries but remain committed to honoring themselves.

In contrast, people who struggle with self-worth may prioritize external validation over their own needs. To be liked or accepted, they may tolerate mistreatment, overcommit, or stay in unhealthy relationships. Nonetheless, establishing boundaries is a form of self-care, not narcissism. It is a declaration that one's own emotions and needs are just as important as those of others.

The Growth Process

For those who struggle with setting boundaries, it is important to recognize that this is a skill that develops over time. Initially, asserting boundaries may feel uncomfortable, particularly for people who have been conditioned to prioritize others over themselves. However, with practice, they begin to internalize the understanding that they are worthy of respect.

Over time, setting boundaries becomes second nature. Saying "no" is no longer seen as risky but as an essential aspect of self-preservation. As self-esteem grows, it becomes easier to end relationships that violate personal boundaries.

Ultimately, boundaries reflect self-worth. They indicate the extent to which a person prioritizes their emotional and physical needs, values their well-being, and respects themselves. Establishing clear, healthy boundaries validates one's values and fosters relationships built on mutual respect and compassion. In contrast, the absence or inadequacy of boundaries often signals challenges with self-esteem. While setting and maintaining boundaries is a lifelong practice, it is one of the most important steps in cultivating a strong sense of self-worth and leading a more fulfilling, healthier life.

Chapter

--- ◆ ---

THE COST OF NOT SETTING BOUNDARIES

The Impact on Your Peace of Mind

Mental health has emerged as a critical concern affecting peoples of all ages and backgrounds in today's fast-paced world. Mental fatigue and tension can result from the constant juggling act that the demands of modern life—both personal and professional—often cause. Yet, a frequently overlooked aspect of preserving mental health is setting and maintaining boundaries. The purpose of this article is to investigate the detrimental effects of failing to establish and maintain boundaries on mental health.

1. Overwhelm and Stress

Neglecting to establish clear boundaries results in a variety of stressors and overwhelming situations:

Overcommitment: Without boundaries, you may become over-dedicated to personal endeavors, social obligations, or work. This can result in an ongoing level of exhaustion and activity.

The absence of boundaries makes it difficult to prioritize tasks and responsibilities effectively. You may find it challenging to distinguish between what is genuinely meaningful and what can be overlooked or disregarded.

Unable to Refuse: The inability to decline is one of the primary causes of tension in boundary-less situations. You may feel compelled to accept every request or invitation, as you are concerned that saying no will disappoint others.

The absence of time boundaries may lead to neglecting personal time for pursuing interests, engaging in self-care, and relaxing. This neglect often leads to chronic stress and a decline in overall well-being.

2. Exhaustion and Burnout

Without clear boundaries, you may experience extreme exhaustion and fatigue. Physical and emotional exhaustion can result from continuously pushing beyond your capabilities without setting clear boundaries around working hours or taking regular breaks.

Paradoxically, the lack of boundaries can decrease productivity. Exhaustion can impede your capacity to concentrate and complete tasks effectively.

Over time, this prolonged strain can negatively impact physical health, resulting in conditions such as insomnia, migraines, and more severe health issues.

3. Effects on Mental Health: Anxiety and depression can be exacerbated by unmanaged stress and exhaustion. It is crucial to acknowledge the correlation between mental well-being and boundaries.

4. Issues with Relationships

Failure to establish boundaries can also hurt your relationships:

Resentment: Continually sacrificing your own needs or aspirations for others can breed resentment. Over time, these feelings can accumulate and cause distress in relationships.

Communication Failure: Misunderstandings may develop in relationships when boundaries and needs are not communicated. Consequently, this may lead to emotional distance and conflict.

Loss of Individuality: When boundaries are absent, you may become entangled in the lives of others, causing you to lose sight of your own unique identity. This can negatively impact both personal and professional relationships.

Toxic Relationships: The absence of boundaries allows manipulative or toxic peoples to exploit your vulnerability; healthy boundaries help prevent such relationships.

Recognizing and establishing boundaries is essential for maintaining healthy and fulfilling relationships, preventing burnout, and supporting overall well-being. Ultimately, boundaries enable you to make conscious decisions about how to invest your time, energy, and resources, thereby enhancing your quality of life.

Common Signs You Need Stronger Boundaries

Healthy boundaries are vital for safeguarding our mental health and emotional well-being. They enable us to establish clear limits and determine what is permissible and impermissible in our interactions and relationships. Nevertheless, identifying when our boundaries are violated is not always straightforward.

1. Feeling Overwhelmed

When you start feeling emotionally drained and distressed after specific interactions consistently, it's a clear sign that your boundaries are being crossed. Recognizing this is the first step toward taking back control and feeling empowered in your relationships. Understanding when others push past your boundaries and asking for more than you can reasonably give is crucial.

2. Difficulty Expressing Refusal

A clear indication of weak boundaries is the inability to decline requests or demands and the subsequent sense of obligation to respond favorably. Peoples with poor boundaries often fear disappointing others or being perceived as self-centered. Learning to say no assertively when necessary is critical to establishing and maintaining healthy boundaries.

3. Consistently Seeking Approval

Frequently seeking validation from others may point to fragile boundaries. This reliance on external approval can fuel self-doubt and reduce confidence. Developing a healthy sense of self-worth and reducing dependence on others for validation are essential to establishing firm boundaries.

4. Feeling Obligated to Manage the Emotions of Others

Poor boundaries are often indicated by assuming responsibility for others' emotions or attempting to resolve their issues. It is crucial to remember that you are not responsible for the emotional well-being of others. Each person is responsible for their own emotions and behaviors.

5. Neglecting Your Requirements

Your needs are just as important as anyone else's. If you consistently put others' needs before your own, it may be a sign of weak boundaries. Neglecting self-care in favor of meeting others' demands can lead to resentment and exhaustion. By establishing boundaries, you prioritize your well-being and demonstrate the value and importance you deserve.

6. Accepting Disrespectful Conduct

Allowing others to disparage or belittle you without repercussion clearly indicates that your boundaries require improvement. Establishing clear expectations for how you wish to be treated and respecting your values to foster healthy relationships is essential.

7. Difficulty Expressing Emotions

Struggling to communicate your emotions or articulate your needs can reflect inadequate boundaries. Healthy boundaries require candid and transparent communication, enabling you to articulate your feelings and express your desires and needs assertively.

8. Experiencing Shame for Scheduling Personal Time

Feeling guilty or embarrassed when you take time for yourself is a clear sign that your boundaries need strengthening. Remember, self-care is not selfish; it is a necessary part of maintaining a healthy life. Don't let the fear of being seen as self-centered prevent you from taking care of yourself.

9. Permitting Others to Assess Your Value

Allowing others to establish your value signals that your boundaries require reinforcement. It is essential to acknowledge that your self-worth should not be contingent upon the opinions or judgments of others. Establishing boundaries enables you to develop your value and worth.

10. Feeling Compelled to Justify Your Decisions

Consistently feeling the need to defend your actions or justify your decisions to others may indicate weak personal boundaries. While being accountable is crucial, you are responsible for your own decisions and choices and are not obligated to provide an explanation or justification to anyone unless you choose to do so.

11. Difficulty Establishing Priorities

The inability to establish priorities and the persistent feeling of being pulled in multiple directions may indicate the need to set more effective boundaries. By establishing distinct boundaries, you can allocate your time, energy, and resources more efficiently according to your values and needs.

12. Experiencing Frustration and Resentment

Persistent feelings of frustration or resentment toward others often suggest that your boundaries are being overlooked or violated. It is crucial to examine these emotions and determine whether they result from unclear or undefined boundaries. Establishing and enforcing healthy boundaries can help alleviate these negative emotions.

The initial step in establishing more fulfilling and healthier relationships is identifying signs that suggest a need for firmer boundaries. If you recognize any of the indicators described in this article, it is time to prioritize your health and establish more effective boundaries. Remember that establishing boundaries is not egotistical; it is essential for preserving your emotional and mental well-being. Begin nurturing respectful and honorable boundaries that align with your needs and values by engaging in self-care, assertiveness, and self-awareness.

When the Fear of Discomfort Holds You Back

Why do some people experience dread at the thought of disappointing others?

The anxiety associated with disappointing others can be attributed to a variety of psychological and social factors:

1. Expectations of Society

People have unique perspectives on societal expectations that govern success, achievement, and standards. They are motivated to adhere to these standards and avoid social disapproval.

2. Parental Expectations and Upbringing

The fear of disappointing parents can significantly shape a person's experiences. Past encounters with rejection, disappointment, or criticism can also contribute to developing a fear of letting others down.

3. Need for Validation

For some people, external validation is the source of self-worth. The dread is, therefore, associated with the potential loss of that approval.

4. The Pursuit of Perfection

Those with perfectionistic tendencies often worry about making mistakes. As they endeavor to achieve perfection, they experience anxiety due to the fear of falling short of their own or others' expectations.

5. Awareness of Your Obligations

People with a strong sense of responsibility for the welfare of others may be apprehensive about disappointing those they care for. This fear results from the belief that they are responsible for the pleasure or prosperity of others.

Ways to Overcome the Fear of Disappointing Others

Your mental well-being may be compromised if you grapple with this apprehension:

1. Dispute Excessive Expectations

Challenge any unattainable standards or expectations that you have imposed on yourself. Recognize that everyone makes mistakes and strive for realistic and achievable goals, as perfectionism frequently exacerbates the fear of disappointment.

2. Establish Healthy Boundaries

Acquire the ability to establish and communicate healthy boundaries. Acknowledge and honor your limitations and requirements. Setting clear boundaries can prevent overcommitment and alleviate anxiety about failing to meet others' expectations.

3. Demonstrate Self-Compassion

Develop self-compassion by treating yourself with kindness and empathy, particularly during moments of perceived failure. It is essential to recognize that everyone makes errors, and through self-compassion, you can approach challenges with a more optimistic and supportive mindset.

4. Enhance Communication Abilities

Enhance your capacity to articulate your thoughts, emotions, and requirements in an assertive and transparent manner. Effective communication fosters stronger, more understanding relationships, reducing the fear of disappointment often associated with potential misunderstandings.

5. Acknowledge the Presence of Imperfections

Adopt the notion that errors are an inherent aspect of the human experience and that perfection is unattainable. Accepting imperfection can mitigate the fear of disappointing others, enabling personal development and resilience in the face of setbacks.

Chapter

---◆---

IDENTIFYING YOUR BOUNDARIES

Assessing Your Needs and Limits

Detecting Emotional Energy Drains

Establishing boundaries begins with assessing what causes an person to feel drained and what is needed to feel secure and respected. Many people feel drained or resentful throughout their day, often without fully understanding why. Self-awareness and a willingness to assess patterns in relationships, environments, and commitments are essential for identifying these sources of emotional depletion. This process entails acknowledging personal needs—not just in general, but specifically in what elicits feelings of safety and appreciation.

Monitoring Emotional Responses Throughout the Day

One effective way to identify energy drains is by tracking emotional responses during the day. Insight can be gained by observing when feelings of frustration, anxiety, or exhaustion arise and which tasks or interactions cause them. For some, this may stem from social interactions that leave them feeling unheard, or environments in which they continually overextend themselves. For others, the depletion may originate from work expectations, domestic responsibilities, or internal pressures, such as perfectionism or people-pleasing tendencies.

Identifying Patterns of Fear and Avoidance

Recurring feelings of apprehension or aversion often indicate areas where boundaries are needed. If certain commitments, relationships, or obligations consistently cause emotional distress, the issue may not lie with the task or the person but rather with the lack of boundaries. For example, some people may enjoy helping others but feel anxious when they are expected to be constantly available. The underlying problem is not generosity but the absence of boundaries that protect their well-being.

Determining the Qualities of Safety and Respect

After identifying depleting factors, the subsequent phase is understanding what fosters a sense of safety and respect. Though subjective, common needs include personal space, declining without remorse, being treated with respect, and having time to recharge without external pressure. People who regularly feel exhausted or unappreciated often haven't clearly defined or communicated their needs.

Utilizing Self-Advocacy to Strengthen Boundaries

Self-advocacy is inextricably linked to safety and respect. Those who are respected tend to assert their needs clearly and consistently— explicitly or through actions. This does not necessitate substantial changes; instead, it involves subtle, deliberate modifications in communication and conduct. It could mean setting clearer expectations at work, limiting time spent with specific people, or modifying commitments to reflect current capacity.

Ensuring Consistent Awareness of Needs

Evaluating what is necessary for security and respect—and what is draining—is an ongoing process. As life circumstances change, so do personal boundaries. The goal is not to eliminate every challenge or difficult interaction but to create an environment that supports your vitality and well-being. The better you understand your needs, the more intentionally you can shape your life around your self-worth.

What Boundaries Look Like for You

What does it mean for you to establish boundaries?

Boundaries are deeply personal and can vary widely. What feels acceptable to one person may be perceived as intrusive or overwhelming by another. Understanding your own boundaries begins with self-reflection on what feels comfortable across different areas of life, including work, social settings, relationships, and personal time. By clearly defining these boundaries, you can cultivate self-respect, emotional safety, and balance in your daily interactions.

Identifying Your Limitations

Recognizing your limitations is the foundation of healthy boundaries. This includes comprehending your physical, mental, and emotional thresholds. For instance, some people feel drained by prolonged social interactions and require time to recuperate. Others flourish in highly social environments but require emotional distance in specific relationships. Awareness of what triggers distress or fatigue is the first step to setting meaningful boundaries.

Diverse Boundaries

Boundaries can manifest in various forms, including physical, emotional, time-based, and digital boundaries. Personal space and physical contact are essential physical boundaries. While some people are at ease with embraces, others prefer a handshake or no physical contact. Emotional boundaries involve protecting your emotions and energy, such as refraining from emotionally draining conversations or avoiding excessive criticism. Time-based boundaries are established to prevent exhaustion by setting restrictions on personal responsibilities, social engagements, and work commitments. Digital boundaries may involve setting the right time and manner for interacting with messages, social media, or online platforms to protect your mental health.

Communicating Boundaries Clearly

Effective boundaries require clear communication. It's not enough to know your limits—others must understand them too. For example, communicating to a friend, "I require some time to myself after work to relax before making plans," or informing a colleague, "I refrain from responding to emails after 7 PM," establishes explicit boundaries. Boundaries do not have to be rigid or severe; they can be communicated with confidence and compassion.

Modifying Boundaries as Required

Boundaries evolve; as you grow or circumstances shift, what once worked may need adjustment. For instance, someone who previously thrived in a fast-paced, always-available work environment may, in the future, recognize the need for a more robust work-life balance. Consistently reevaluating boundaries ensures they remain relevant and supportive of your needs and well-being.

Boundaries Respected Without Shame

Many people feel remorse when enforcing boundaries, especially if they are accustomed to prioritizing the comfort of others over their own needs. Nevertheless, establishing boundaries is not a matter of selfishness but self-respect and self-care. Saying no to exhausting situations, requesting space, or withdrawing from others does not imply rejecting them. Those who genuinely respect and care for you will understand and honor these boundaries.

Developing a Life That Is Consistent with Your Requirements

By establishing and maintaining personal boundaries, people can create a life aligned with their values, needs, and well-being. Instead of experiencing overextension, resentment, or overwhelm, they can foster relationships and environments that support personal growth. Understanding what boundaries look like on a personal level empowers you to navigate life with confidence, self-respect, and a deeper sense of fulfillment.

To lead a healthy, grounded life, it is essential to understand and respect your body. In times of stress, transition, or crisis, we often disconnect from our emotions and dismiss physical symptoms. We retreat into our minds, where we endeavor to regulate our lives. It is possible to reconnect with and rediscover our vitality by listening to our bodies, which provides a pathway to greater stability and pleasure in life while simultaneously reducing anxiety, depression, and exhaustion. It enables us to establish a secure foundation upon which to rely during difficult times and circumstances by allowing us to anchor our experiences in physical sensations, thereby strengthening our connection to our identity.

We Are a Combination of Body and Mind

As human beings, we are both body and psyche. Yet, our society often values cognition over perception and somatic attention. All emotions, thoughts, and actions occur within the body. Our bodies are the stage upon which all of our experiences transpire. The mental and the physical are inextricably linked. We experience a sense of belonging in our bodies and our lives when we acquire the ability to interpret our physical experiences.

We have all learned to disregard our bodies' signals. We are accustomed to hearing our thoughts, which leaves us "up in our heads" and with little awareness of the world below our shoulders. Our minds frequently persuade us that there is a more significant alternative, even when our bodies' signals do not align with our objectives. Alternatively, we have an idea of what we should be experiencing, regardless of whether it aligns with our actual experiences. We do not wish to be ill, yet we neglect thirst, delay sleep when fatigued, and fail to breathe adequately during periods of intense emotion. We exert ourselves when we are genuinely in need of a vacation. When we need a conversation with a trusted friend, we close down and isolate ourselves. Relearning to observe the body takes intentional practice.

Listen to Your Body

Cultivate awareness of the present moment, as this will reduce the likelihood of becoming disoriented in the future or entangled in the past. Body-based perception, sensation, and thinking enable us to observe our truth regardless of the opinions of our rational mind. We cannot merely assume that we are grounded; we must experience it through our physical sensations.

Identify the appropriate words to accurately convey the physical aspects of your emotions and experiences. This method converts overwhelming experiences into a somatic process. Rather than being bewildered by an incomprehensible emotional state, you will acquire the ability to focus on sensations such as a clenched abdomen, rigid shoulders, shallow respiration, and a tense larynx. This clarity often softens emotional intensity and improves communication about your feelings and needs.

"Feel" your emotions—to be in contact with and experience the energy and physical impulses they generate within your body without reflexively reacting to them. Emotions can't be reasoned away—they must be felt. This builds inner trust and allows you to support yourself during emotional storms.

Comprehend the intricacies of your experience. In our daily lives, we often have limited access to only certain aspects of our emotional environment. The body holds more insight than our conscious awareness. Tuning into it expands emotional access and strengthens intuition, leading to wiser decisions and more aligned actions.

Avoid being influenced by your emotions and experiences. Emotions are involuntary, and we can influence them when we recognize they are a collection of physical sensations. You can contract or expand, retain or continue breathing, tense or relax your muscles, remain still or move, and change can occur.

Practices for Mind-Body Connection

Listening to your body is often counterintuitive. We naturally avoid experiences that we dislike or find uncomfortable. Yet listening to our bodies involves turning toward those experiences and the physical sensations they evoke, staying with them, and becoming intrigued.

Listening to your body is not about increasing physical activity, improving your diet, or taking a daily walk. It is not a tool but a principle. It is a state of being where we become more attuned to our emotions and sensations, allowing our bodies to inform our minds. This continuous, lifelong practice touches every aspect of our lives. As you grow and your life experiences deepen, so will your ability to listen more profoundly.

To listen to your body is to be receptive to its unique language of sensations. To do this, we must pause, quiet our inner stream of thoughts, calm ourselves, and focus on what our bodies are experiencing. We must transition from thinking to sensing. For many, observing their breath facilitates their connection to their somatic experience. Others may need movement or physical contact to more accurately identify what they're feeling.

Chapter

◆

SETTING BOUNDARIES WITH CONFIDENCE

How to Communicate Your Boundaries Clearly

Despite the widespread understanding of boundaries and their frequent discussion in self-help literature, many people have not been taught how to communicate them effectively. Some have even been conditioned not to express boundaries at all. Boundaries can result in strained relationships filled with dissatisfaction and resentment when left unspoken.

Boundaries are the structures that help us feel safe, respected, valued, and cared for in relationships. Since boundaries vary from person to person, identifying them requires attentiveness to moments of discomfort, frustration, or feelings of being taken advantage of. For example, if a loved one frequently interrupts during conversations, it may evoke feelings of disrespect, frustration, and undervaluation. If such boundaries are not communicated, unresolved tension can lead to resentment and emotional distance, often without the other person realizing the impact of their actions.

Establishing boundaries empowers people to express their needs openly, fostering intimacy, respect, and authenticity. Using the earlier example of frequent interruptions, setting a boundary might involve saying:

"I feel inferior when I'm interrupted. I want to feel like an equal in this conversation."

Sometimes, simply stating the boundary is enough. In other cases, reinforcement is necessary as the other person adjusts to the new expectations. A more action-based approach might be:

"We've discussed how interruptions make me feel undervalued. Because I care about our relationship and this is important to me, I will pause the conversation when I'm interrupted until you recognize it, and then we can continue."

Using "I" statements helps maintain a collaborative and non-confrontational tone. Rather than saying, "You're always late," which may trigger defensiveness, one might say, "I feel unimportant when I'm kept waiting." This keeps the focus on your personal experience, encouraging dialogue rather than conflict.

Steps for Implementing Boundaries

Begin with the Basics

Once someone understands the importance of boundaries, they may feel compelled to set them in every area of life. However, like any new habit, boundaries require time and patience. Introducing them gradually allows both parties to adjust without feeling overwhelmed. Drastic changes can unsettle relational dynamics and create confusion or resistance.

Anticipate Pushback

Resistance is a natural response to new boundaries. While the boundary-setter may have harbored their feelings for a long time, it's often new information to the other party. For example, if someone has interrupted their partner for years, they may not realize how disruptive it feels. Their reaction may involve mixed emotions, possibly leading to discussions about their boundaries.

Remain Consistent and Compassionate

Consistency is key to reinforcing boundaries. Gently reminding others and following through with stated actions—such as pausing a conversation when interrupted—helps establish new norms. However, it is equally essential to maintain kindness and patience. Frustration may arise, but remembering that both parties care about the relationship can ease the process. A calm voice, mindful breathing, and continued mutual respect support smoother transitions.

As someone gains confidence in identifying and upholding their boundaries, they foster healthier and more fulfilling relationships. Expressing personal needs and ensuring they are acknowledged reduces resentment and emotional distance while encouraging deeper connections built on honesty, mutual respect, and clarity.

The Power of Saying No

Saying "no" can be liberating and empowering for some but intimidating or unpleasant for others. Social norms often suggest that saying no is rude or inconsiderate. As a result, we may feel obligated to agree to things we'd rather avoid to remain socially accepted.

Yet, there are clear advantages to saying "no." It supports self-care, builds confidence, and reinforces mental health stability through healthy boundaries. Although it may be intimidating to decline an offer, there are methods to make the process easier.

Alternative Methods of Expressing Refusal

The first step in harnessing the power of no is finding a way to express it authentically and comfortably. One useful technique is the sandwich method, which places a potentially negative response between two positive or supportive statements.

For example:

"Thank you for the invitation. I appreciate your thoughtfulness, but I won't be able to attend. I would still love to connect and will check my schedule to find a time that works for us."

Additionally, consider the rationale behind your decision not to participate in an activity. Is it due to your reluctance to attend an event with specific people? Is the pandemic causing you to feel uneasy about venturing out? Are you feeling fatigued and needing a break from your hectic schedule? Reflecting on your emotions and identifying behavioral patterns can also contribute to your confidence in declining.

It is also crucial to remember that declining an offer while providing alternatives that are more suitable for your requirements can effectively leverage the power of no. Your decisions significantly impact your time and energy, and your needs are substantial.

Setting Healthy Boundaries

We all play various roles—at work, in childcare, through social obligations, and within family dynamics. These roles can sometimes challenge our ability to establish and maintain boundaries. Understanding yourself and uncovering your innate potential is essential to your overall well-being.

It can be beneficial to establish boundaries around personal objectives. For instance, if you're working toward a more balanced work-life dynamic, you might decline calls or meetings outside your regular work hours by employing some of the strategies above.

Even in limited contexts, such as social media, expressing a yes or no to an inquiry can effectively maintain boundaries. Recognize that not all people are friends, and it is acceptable to decline a friend request. If certain posts make you uncomfortable, curating your feed can help. These small steps can significantly boost your mental well-being.

Boundaries are also flexible when necessary. Permit yourself to reevaluate them over time, considering both the advantages and disadvantages. Remember: boundaries are not required to be permanent.

Different Types of Self-Care

For some, saying no is a form of self-care—especially while learning to establish boundaries. Beyond declining requests, you may also wish to incorporate supplementary self-care activities that help recharge your energy and promote emotional resilience. For example, turning down an invitation—even one you'd normally accept—can allow you to conserve energy for the next priority or meaningful relationship.

Positive affirmations are another effective self-care tool, helping you focus on your accomplishments and personal strengths. Engaging in creative pursuits, including art, dance, meditation, and yoga, is also a valuable way to care for your mind and body.

It is crucial to find ways to nurture a healthy mindset. Our beliefs can significantly impact our success and sense of contentment. Studies have demonstrated that self-care can improve overall health and relationships, with benefits that last for years.

Recognizing Critical Indicators

Being able to express yourself and stand steadfast in your decisions can be extremely empowering; however, staying aware of potential warning signs is important. Isolating behaviors, withdrawal, loss of interest in usual activities, or feelings of worthlessness may indicate that your well-being is being compromised. These could signal a severe mental health concern, such as depression. If setting boundaries leaves you feeling lonely or emotionally withdrawn, it may be time to speak with a mental health professional.

In general, there is no definitive method for declining an offer. Self-expression is personal, and trying different approaches can help you discover what works best for you. Remember: it is impossible to satisfy all people—and trying to do so often leads to unintended outcomes. Let your innate confidence shine through in your decisions and boundary-setting.

Chapter

---◆---

BOUNDARIES IN RELATIONSHIPS

Boundaries with Family

Family dynamics can be complex. You can't choose your family, and they can be either the most challenging or the finest aspects of your life. They are perpetually present. Navigating these relationships—especially when they are toxic, overbearing, or cause conflict—can be difficult.

Establishing healthy boundaries is key to maintaining balance and protecting your peace. Setting boundaries with family members, whether they are parents, siblings, or extended family, is a skill everyone should acquire.

Strategies for Establishing Boundaries with Your Family

Establishing clear boundaries with your family can be challenging, but being prepared equips you with the necessary resources to maintain safety and respect in these relationships.

Practice

If you've felt disrespected or overwhelmed by toxic family behavior, you are likely at a point where clear boundaries are necessary. In their presence, you may tend to cower or feel vulnerable if such behavior occurs frequently. When people challenge your limits, declining or advocating for yourself can be transformative.

Even if you tend to people-please or fear disappointing others, you can still say no. Practicing setting and adhering to your boundaries in advance can help you feel more prepared, willing, and capable of enforcing them.

Recognize That Your Needs Are Significant

Before setting boundaries with family, acknowledge that your needs are valid, significant, and genuine. It is common to feel anxious about possibly upsetting a family member when discussing boundaries. However, setting boundaries is not harmful—in fact, it fosters healthier, more respectful relationships. Your needs are just as important as anyone else's.

Firmness and Compassion

For your boundaries to be respected, you must express them clearly and firmly. However, firmness does not require callousness. Often, a calm, patient, and kind approach yields better results. Firmness means standing your ground while maintaining your values and integrity.

Be Forthright

Discussing boundaries can be uncomfortable, especially with family. The most effective method is to be forthright. Express your expectations honestly without leaving room for ambiguity. Let others know what behaviors are acceptable and which are not.

Remove Yourself When Necessary

You are never obligated to remain in a toxic or unsafe space. If your boundaries are not being honored, you have every right to leave. While negotiation might be an option, in long-standing difficult situations, stepping away entirely may be the healthiest choice. You don't owe anyone an apology or explanation unless you choose to offer one.

Recognize Your Authority

Recognizing that you are responsible for your own life is a significant component of establishing healthy boundaries. Once you've communicated your limits, know that you have the strength and authority to uphold them. No one can force you to feel a certain way or act against your will. It is reasonable to expect your boundaries to be respected—even by family.

Display Assertiveness

Being assertive can be difficult, especially with family. Developing rules with senior family members can feel unfamiliar, as we are frequently taught to be deferential. Assertiveness, however, does not constitute disrespect. Confidently advocating for yourself is both acceptable and often necessary.

Boundaries at Work

Interpersonal boundaries define emotional, physical, and mental space. They guide our interactions, dictate the extent to which we are willing to give or receive, and set the standard for acceptable behavior. Healthy workplace boundaries—whether explicit or implicit—are essential for respectful and productive relationships.

Practical Strategies for Workplace Boundaries

1. **Communicate Clearly**

   Be transparent about your professional boundaries. Clearly articulate areas where you are and are not comfortable.

   Example: "I prefer not to be contacted on weekends except in emergencies. Please contact me during business hours if needed. Explicit examples of emergencies can also help avoid ambiguity."

2. **Decline When Necessary**

   It is permissible to refuse additional duties when overextended. Politely prioritize your workload.

   Example: "I appreciate the opportunity; however, my current workload will not permit me to undertake this project. Can we revisit this at a later date?"

3. **Establish Overtime Boundaries**

   Prevent overextension by setting limits on working late or bringing work home.

   Example: "I understand that X is important. Can we extend the deadline to ensure both priorities are addressed effectively? If not, which should I deprioritize?"

4. **Manage Interruptions**

   Set specific times for focused work and inform colleagues of your availability.

   Example: "I allocate 'focus time' daily from 10:00 a.m. to 12:00 p.m. Please refrain from scheduling meetings or interruptions during this time."

5. **Use Technology Mindfully**

Limit work-related communications outside designated hours.

Example: "I will not review work emails after 7 p.m. Contact me via text or phone for urgent matters. Please clarify what qualifies as urgent."

6. **Delegate Responsibilities**

Monitor your workload and delegate tasks when appropriate.

Example: "I trust your ability to manage this task, and I am assigning responsibility for organizing the meeting to you."

7. **Define Acceptable Conduct**

Maintain a professional and respectful environment.

Example: "Let's keep discussions professional and avoid personal comments."

8. **Seek Support**

Consult supervisors or HR when encountering boundary challenges.

Example: "I'm struggling to manage my workload. Can we discuss strategies to improve productivity through boundary-setting?"

9. **Practice Self-Compassion**

Assess your emotional and mental state before taking on new responsibilities. Your capacity may fluctuate weekly, and that's acceptable.

Example: Pause each morning to evaluate your state before responding to new requests.

Enhancing Personal Boundaries

Personal boundaries define limits around your body, emotions, finances, physical spaces, and digital presence. You choose what information to share, just as others decide what they share with you. Trust and respect are essential; no partner should pressure you to redefine your boundaries, and you have the right to decide what is appropriate for you at any given time.

Boundaries enable you to determine how you wish to be treated while respecting your partner's limits. Types of boundaries in personal relationships include:

Digital Boundaries

Define comfort levels around computers, social media, mobile phones, and online profiles. Clarify expectations regarding communication and account access. You are not obligated to share login credentials, even with a trusted partner.

Physical Boundaries

Set limits regarding your body, home, and personal spaces. Communicate comfort levels with physical touch, intimacy, and public displays of affection. Regulate emotions to allow rational discussion during conflicts. Physical harm is never acceptable.

Financial Boundaries

Determine comfort levels regarding income, bank accounts, credit cards, and other financial matters. Discuss shared expenses without disclosing every financial detail. Your financial privacy is valid.

Emotional Boundaries

Manage trust, vulnerability, and emotional sharing. Determine what emotional support is suitable, and establish boundaries gradually.

Maintain emotional independence alongside your partner while nurturing mutual trust.

A healthy, balanced relationship requires **emotional, financial, physical, and digital boundaries**. Boundaries safeguard your well-being and foster mutual respect, trust, and understanding. They are reciprocal, flexible, and may evolve as you grow within your relationship.

Chapter

--- ♦ ---

THE BENEFITS OF HEALTHY BOUNDARIES

Boundaries to Improve Your Well-Being

Establishing clear boundaries benefits you and those around you. When you are unambiguous about your boundaries, others will understand your limitations and recognize what you are and are not willing to accept, thereby modifying their behavior. People who disregard your boundaries may not be the best fit for your life.

Setting healthy boundaries can help you:

1. Develop a higher sense of self-worth

2. Obtain a comprehensive understanding of your identity, aspirations, values, and beliefs

3. Concentrate on your health and well-being

4. Improve your emotional and mental health
5. Prevent exhaustion

Strategies for Enhancing Your Well-Being Through the Use of Boundaries

The most effective approach to establishing boundaries is through direct, candid, and transparent feedback regarding your limitations. Try the following suggestions:

Express your ideas. When discussing your emotions and thoughts with another person, it is essential to be forthright yet considerate. It is permissible to take a moment to collect yourself before and after the discussion. However, do not allow this to be an excuse to suppress or avoid expressing your emotions.

Do not make assumptions or guesses about the emotions of others. Assumptions can result in numerous misunderstandings within a relationship. Even if you feel you have a profound understanding of someone and could infer their thoughts, it is always preferable to inquire rather than speculate.

Adhere to your statements. When you set boundaries but fail to enforce them, others may perceive this as permission to overstep them. Do not make any exceptions to your boundaries without carefully considering the implications. Otherwise, you may be compelled to compromise on matters that are not to your liking.

Accept accountability for your conduct. Consider the choices you have made in a relationship and whether they may have contributed to the situation, rather than placing blame or lamenting the problem or how you are feeling.

Recognize when it is time to progress. You have the right to express your preferences regarding treatment in a relationship; however, you are not accountable for your partner's emotions or communication. Everyone deserves to be treated with respect and equity. If someone cannot respect your boundaries, it may be time to terminate the relationship.

Your Mental Health and the Limits of Boundaries

It can be challenging to prioritize yourself; however, the present moment presents an opportunity to do so. Establishing boundaries can be a valuable skill that enhances your relationships and supports your future recovery.

Boundaries facilitate self-awareness and healthier relationships. They are crucial for self-care and prioritizing yourself. If you are experiencing feelings of insecurity, resentment, or dissatisfaction in your relationships, or if you feel you are being taken advantage of or losing your sense of self, it is essential to consider whether you have problematic boundaries and establish healthy ones.

It is also crucial to acknowledge that boundaries are not a substitute for mental health treatment, despite their potential to be an effective instrument for managing and shifting emotions.

Improved Relationships

Enhanced Relationships: The Role of Healthy Boundaries in the Development of More Balanced and Satisfying Connections

Healthy boundaries are crucial for maintaining mutual respect, understanding, and emotional well-being in any romantic, familial, professional, or platonic relationship. The limits of permissible behavior are defined by boundaries, which clarify what is and is not appropriate within a relationship. You establish and maintain these boundaries to develop a foundation of trust, balance, and a deeper connection.

Comprehending Healthy Boundaries

Healthy boundaries establish guidelines for how you interact with others while safeguarding your own emotional, mental, and physical well-being. They help differentiate personal needs from others' expectations, fostering self-respect and autonomy. Without clear boundaries, relationships may become burdensome, depleting, or even toxic, leading to misunderstandings, frustration, and resentment.

Depending on the nature of the relationship, boundaries may differ. For instance, romantic partnerships may encompass personal independence, communication preferences, or emotional space. Meanwhile, they may pertain to confidentiality, support, and reverence for time in friendships. In professional environments, they contribute to the preservation of workplace ethics, professionalism, and work-life balance.

The Advantages of Healthy Boundaries

1. Increasing Mutual Respect

One of the most significant advantages of establishing boundaries is fostering mutual respect. When you communicate your requirements and limitations clearly and concisely, you develop the expectation that your feelings, time, and energy are valuable. This results in relationships where both parties demonstrate consideration, concern, and respect for each other's boundaries.

For example, a respectful acquaintance or companion will honor an your request for uninterrupted work time by refraining from interrupting them repeatedly. This mutual comprehension fortifies the relationship's foundation and prevents conflicts.

2. Mitigating Stress and Resentment

Stress and resentment are frequently the result of unclear or nonexistent boundaries. Over time, frustration builds when people feel compelled to compromise their comfort or overextend themselves to satisfy others. This can lead to emotional exhaustion, fatigue, and strained relationships.

You prevent the accumulation of resentment by establishing clear boundaries. For instance, you consistently consent to social engagements despite needing personal relaxation which may eventually lead to exhaustion and irritability. Setting a boundary, such as declining invitations when necessary, is beneficial for maintaining equilibrium and preventing resentment toward others.

3. Promoting Transparent Communication

Healthy boundaries promote open and honest communication, enabling you to express your needs, feelings, and expectations without fear of conflict. Rather than suppressing emotions or engaging in passive-aggressive behavior, clear boundaries promote direct and constructive conversations.

For instance, you may articulate, "I am disappointed when our plans are repeatedly canceled. I would appreciate more consistency and value our time together," rather than feeling irritated by a friend who frequently cancels plans at the last minute. These conversations foster problem-solving and understanding rather than the retention of unspoken grievances.

4. Enhancing Physical and Emotional Health

You develop a sense of self-worth and empowerment when you prioritize your emotional and physical well-being by establishing healthy boundaries. Personal space, self-care, and sufficient rest become indispensable components of life, leading to improved mental health and reduced anxiety.

Additionally, boundaries help prevent toxic dynamics and emotional manipulation. For example, you can safeguard yourself from toxic relationships and preserve your self-esteem by acknowledging and addressing emotional gaslighting or guilt-tripping behaviors.

5. Promoting Balance and Reciprocity

Balanced relationships thrive on reciprocity, where both parties contribute and respect each other's boundaries. Without this balance, a relationship may become one-sided, with one person consistently giving while the other receives.

For example, dissatisfaction may arise from an imbalance in which an acquaintance consistently requests emotional support but is unavailable when this support is needed. Establishing healthy boundaries ensures that both parties feel equally valued and supported, thereby promoting equity.

Establishing Healthy Relationship Boundaries

Although it is essential to comprehend the significance of boundaries, your practical implementation requires patience and practice. The following are crucial measures for establishing and maintaining boundaries:

1. **Determine Personal Requirements and Limitations**
   To determine what constitutes a relationship that is both respectful and comfortable, you should consider your emotional, mental, and physical needs. Recognizing patterns of distress or frustration can help gain insight into the necessity of boundaries.

2. **Communicate with Clarity and Confidence**
   Misunderstandings are prevented by articulating boundaries in an assertive and transparent manner. Rather than stating, "You never give me space," utilizing "I" statements, such as "I need some alone time in the evenings to recharge," fosters constructive dialogue and reduces defensiveness.

3. **Consistently Enforce Boundaries**
   Setting a boundary is only effective if it is consistently enforced. You should reinforce your boundaries by taking appropriate actions, such as withdrawing from situations where their limits are not respected.

4. **Show Respect for the Boundaries of Others**

In the same way that you establish your boundaries, you must also respect the boundaries of others. Mutual respect and stronger relationships are fostered by acknowledging and respecting another person's limits.

5. **Modify the Boundaries as Required**

Boundaries may need to be reevaluated and modified as relationships evolve. Ensuring that both parties remain comfortable and valued necessitates open communication regarding changing requirements.

Setting and maintaining healthy boundaries is essential to establishing and sustaining harmonious, satisfying relationships. They foster mutual respect, reduce tension, facilitate open and honest communication, and enhance overall well-being. You establish more rewarding, healthier, and more profound relationships with others by comprehending, establishing, and enforcing boundaries. Boundaries are not set to create distance; they are established to cultivate emotional harmony, trust, and respect in all relationships.

Personal Growth and Self-Respect

The Significance of Establishing Limitations

Establishing boundaries is a crucial aspect of cultivating self-awareness and maintaining overall well-being. Burnout and dissatisfaction often stem from your inability to express your needs, say no, or protect your energy. Nevertheless, you develop a more profound comprehension of your identity, needs, and interactions with the world by establishing unambiguous boundaries.

Boundaries are instrumental in defining permissible and intolerable conduct in various domains, including personal time, work, and relationships. They can be categorized as physical, emotional, intellectual, or time-management-related. By establishing boundaries, you create a space for introspection, enabling you to align your actions with your genuine values and priorities.

Explicating Personal Values

You engage in self-reflection that clarifies personal values when you establish and enforce boundaries. Deeply held beliefs and priorities are revealed by understanding what is tolerable and unacceptable.

For instance, distress with excessive work demands may indicate a strong appreciation for work-life balance. Recognizing these priorities enables you to make informed decisions aligned with your authentic selves, reducing internal conflict and increasing overall satisfaction.

Identifying Emotional Triggers

Emotional responses to boundary violations often highlight unmet needs or unresolved issues. Feelings of frustration, anxiety, or sorrow indicate that something significant is being jeopardized when someone violates a boundary. Observing these reactions can provide you with a deeper understanding of your emotional landscape and help identify areas that require healing or adjustment. This process fosters increased self-awareness and enables the development of strategies to protect emotional well-being.

Developing Self-Respect and Confidence

Self-respect and self-worth are reinforced by setting and enforcing boundaries. Standing firm on your personal limits shows that your needs and emotions are important, whereas allowing others to disregard those limits can lead to resentment and exhaustion. Over time, this practice fosters self-esteem and confidence, empowering people to advocate for themselves in various circumstances.

Enhancing Decision-Making and Intuition

Another significant advantage of establishing boundaries is the ability to rely on your intuition. You may suppress your inner voice to avoid conflict or satisfy others, which can result in feelings of dissatisfaction and a disconnection from your genuine requirements. When you respect your boundaries, you strengthen your connection to your impulses, leading to decisions that more accurately reflect your desires than external pressures. This enhances overall decision-making abilities and fosters greater self-confidence.

Identification of Personal Needs

Boundaries also help you to more accurately identify your personal needs. You may struggle to express your needs due to a lack of articulation. Boundaries offer a structure for identifying the essential components of a sense of balance, fulfillment, and safety.

For instance, when specific interactions consistently result in you feeling depleted, emotional requirement becomes more apparent. Exhaustion or tension may indicate the need for relationships grounded in mutual respect and encouragement, especially if spending time with specific people triggers these emotions. Setting boundaries against detrimental influences prioritizes emotional well-being, resulting in a more satisfying social atmosphere.

Establishing the Expectations of a Relationship

Another essential component of boundary-setting is establishing relationship expectations. Healthy relationships in all aspects of life, such as familial interactions, romantic partnerships, and friendships, are fostered by understanding what behaviors are permissible and what are not. Setting boundaries around dishonesty or manipulation ensures that relationships align with your needs if open communication is a personal priority. Boundaries also foster mutual respect by creating distinct guidelines for behavior, which in turn reduces misunderstandings and conflicts.

Upholding a Healthy Work-Life Balance

Setting boundaries in professional environments is crucial for long-term well-being, as maintaining a healthy work-life balance can be challenging. People may experience burnout, stress, and decreased job satisfaction when clear boundaries are absent. Recognizing the importance of personal time and leisure is essential for establishing boundaries that support mental and physical health and prevent overwork.

Whether it involves refusing to check emails after work hours or setting strict overtime limits, such boundaries help you maintain a sense of control and balance in your professional life.

Admitting to Your Physical and Mental Limitations

Identifying your mental and physical limits is essential for establishing boundaries. Stress, fatigue, and illness are common consequences for people who push themselves beyond their capacities. Practicing self-awareness and self-care means knowing when to decline obligations that compromise your well-being or when to step back if overburdened. By recognizing their limits, people can create a more sustainable lifestyle, prioritizing activities that align with their energy levels and overall health.

Overcoming Obstacles in Establishing Limitations

Despite the many advantages of establishing boundaries, obstacles often arise. Many people are concerned about being perceived as egotistical or unkind, making it challenging to enforce limits due to the fear of disappointing others. Nevertheless, prioritizing the well-being of others over your own can result in feelings of resentment and frustration. Recognizing that boundary-setting is a vital aspect of self-care can help alleviate this guilt and reinforce the importance of maintaining healthy limits.

Acquiring a Clear Understanding of Needs

You may struggle to establish boundaries due to a lack of clarity about your own needs. Insight can be gained by observing situations that induce distress when uncertainty arises. Journaling about draining or distressing interactions can help identify areas where stronger boundaries are needed. Self-reflection is essential for comprehending your boundaries and devising effective strategies to enforce them.

Confronting Resistance

Another common obstacle in establishing boundaries is opposition from others. Some people may resist or challenge boundaries, especially if they have previously benefited from their absence. Maintaining a firm stance and consistently enforcing boundaries in a calm manner is essential in these situations. Over time, most people learn to respect established boundaries, resulting in more positive interactions and healthier relationships.

Guilt Management

Setting boundaries often brings feelings of guilt, especially for people who are used to prioritizing the needs of others over their own. It can be challenging to regulate this guilt; however, it is essential to remember that safeguarding your health is not selfish. Authentic self-care entails acknowledging and respecting your needs, even if it occasionally requires disappointing others. Boundary-setting becomes more manageable with practice, and the remorse accompanying it tends to diminish over time.

Benefits of Establishing Boundaries in the Long Term

Creating and upholding boundaries has significant long-term advantages. One of the most important is the enhancement of mental health, as establishing distinct boundaries reduces tension, anxiety, and burnout. Boundaries also strengthen relationships by fostering mutual understanding and respect. Consistently maintaining your boundaries strengthens self-esteem and confidence, empowering you to assert your value and advocate for your needs effectively.

Additionally, decision-making is enhanced as you make decisions based on their values rather than external pressures. Overall, establishing boundaries leads to increased life satisfaction by allowing you to live authentically.

To cultivate a deeper and more authentic connection with yourself, you must learn to attend to your own needs and respect your personal boundaries. Establishing boundaries is more than self-care; it is a path to self-empowerment and fulfillment. By adopting this practice and prioritizing personal values and well-being, you can achieve a more balanced, healthy, and satisfying life. The first step involves identifying your boundaries, communicating them clearly, and consistently enforcing them. Through this process, you gain a deeper understanding of yourself, fostering emotional well-being and self-awareness.

CONCLUSION

---◆---

EMBRACING YOUR BOUNDARIES WITH CONFIDENCE

A s you reach the end of ***Lines in the Sand: Building Boundaries with Grace***, remember that establishing and maintaining healthy boundaries is not a one-time event but an ongoing process. It's a continual journey of self-awareness, growth, and self-compassion. By honoring your limits and communicating them with clarity and kindness, you are protecting your well-being and fostering healthier, more respectful relationships with those around you.

The boundaries you set are not walls; they are bridges to living a more authentic, fulfilling life. They allow you to engage with the world on your terms, free from guilt or fear of overextension. Through these boundaries, you will discover the space to nurture your passions, protect your peace, and cultivate meaningful connections.

You have the power to choose your boundaries; by doing so, you choose to live with intention, purpose, and grace. Continue to honor your needs, trust yourself, and remember that setting boundaries is a form of self-love. With the tools and insights you've gained, you are now ready to move forward with confidence, knowing that you are worthy of respect, balance, and the life you desire.

Thank you for allowing me to be a part of your journey toward creating boundaries that honor your authentic self. May your path ahead be one of peace, empowerment, and grace.

REFERENCES

◆

CTSA_Therapy. (2021, March 24). *Listening to your mind and body.*
The Center for Trauma, Stress, and Anxiety Therapy.
https://www.ctsatherapy.com/listening-to-your-mind-and-body/

Guo, J. (2023, June 6). *Boundaries: what they are, what they look
like, and how to set them.* NeuroPeak: Physiotherapy, Occupational
Therapy and Counselling.
https://www.neuropeak.ca/blog/wellness-strategies/boundaries-what-
they-are-what-they-look-like-and-how-to-set-them/

Lcsw-R, J. E. D. (2022, November 10). *How to Set Family
Boundaries: A Therapist's Guide.* Talkspace.
https://www.talkspace.com/blog/family-boundaries/

Love is Respect. (2021, February). *How to create boundaries in
romantic relationships.* Love is Respect.
https://www.loveisrespect.org/resources/creating-boundaries-in-
romantic-relationships/

Nicole, A. (2025). *3 kind, simple & effective ways to communicate
your boundaries | Headspace.* Headspace for Organizations.
https://organizations.headspace.com/blog/3-kind-simple-effective-
ways-to-communicate-your-boundaries

Whitener, S. (2019, December 11). *Council Post: How setting
boundaries Positively Impacts your Self-Esteem.* Forbes.

https://www.forbes.com/councils/forbescoachescouncil/2019/12/11/how-setting-boundaries-positively-impacts-your-self-esteem/

WebMD Editorial Contributors. (2021, March). *Setting boundaries.* WebMD.
https://www.webmd.com/mental-health/setting-boundaries

www.ingramcontent.com/pod-product-compliance
Lightning Source LLC
Chambersburg PA
CBHW060353130626
46553CB00003B/1213